Is There *Anybody* That Can Teach Me How To Read?

Practical Strategies for Dramatically Improving Student Learning

S0-DIH-787

Dr. Sonya Whitaker

Printed in the United States of America. (March 2012). Edited by Ward Weldon, Ph.D. Book Cover Design by Dmitry Pavlovsky.

IBSN 9780985209308

A VERY SPECIAL DEDICATION

The story behind the title of this book, <u>Is There *Anybody* That Can Teach Me How to Read?:</u> is what has changed my life as a professional educator forever.

While serving in the capacity of school administrator, a student was sent to my office after demonstrating negative behavior in class. His behavior disruptions were far too much to bear on this day in particular. I immediately called his mother and asked her to pick him up from school.

The student was prompted to remain in his seat in the office until his parent arrived at the school. Moments later I noticed that the student had not followed my request to remain seated. In fact, he was talking to the school secretary.

At the end of the day, the secretary asked me if I was interested in hearing what the student said to her while standing at her desk. Busy at the time, I responded "Sure." She said he asked: "Is There *Anybody* In This School That Can Teach Me How To Read?"

That moment changed my life forever. To the student that had the courage to challenge me to remain focused on the real reason why I chose the education profession. I thank you.

ACKNOWLEDGEMENTS

I would like to acknowledge my husband Marc and two children, Marc Alan and Jalen Whitaker. You have been a rock solid support system. Thank you for your unwavering love and support.

To my mother and father, Alice and George. You taught me the importance of maintaining a great work ethic and caring about others. I am forever grateful for the sacrifices that the two of you made on my behalf, and I am also grateful to both of my siblings, Tonya and Greg.

A special thank you to the editor of this book. Dr. Ward Weldon. I find it difficult to articulate in writing how grateful and humble I am by the fact that I know you. For many years, you have been my professor, senior advisor, mentor, friend and confidant. I would not be who I am today if I had never met you. My family and I are eternally grateful for the role that you play in my life.

To Dr. James Young of Clark Atlanta University, I could never thank you enough. You have been my number-one cheerleader. Your scholarly advice from the moment that I first stepped a foot on a college campus, throughout my entire professional career has contributed to the success that I experience today.

TABLE OF CONTENTS

Foreword

I write this book while having had the opportunity to serve in the capacities of Published Author, school district Superintendent, Keynote speaker, Workshop Facilitator, Educational consultant, Adjunct Professor, Reading Program Consultant, Director of Literacy, Principal, Assistant Principal and Classroom Teacher. The information gathered and shared in this writing represents not only my findings as a practitioner and researcher: it also represents the voices of teachers from across the entire country that have literally cried out to me in an effort to discover more ways in which they can be effective with their students.

Each time that I think about straying away from the writing of this book, I am reminded of the adult educators that have shared that they are tired and on the brink of seriously considering leaving the teaching profession because they feel that they are not being successful with their students. To those teachers that had the courage to share with me their most intimate thoughts: I thank you. You are the reason that I keep writing even though this is sometimes hard to do. Especially, when I look out of the window of my home office to see my youngest son building a house out of cardboard bricks, I step out for brief moment to be of assistance to him. This is a quick but enjoyable moment for the two of us. I guess I could have actually entitled this book

"Sacrifice." This word most definitely describes the way that I feel about taking the time to articulate my thoughts in writing. I do happen to believe however, that our teachers and students are worth it. I have assurance that someday my two boys will grow to understand that the sacrifice of time made to complete this incredible journey will ultimately result in a better world in which they will reside and make important contributions.

Introduction

Many efforts have been made on the part of teachers and administrators to increase the likelihood that all students experience success to the best of their individual abilities. However, teachers are indicating that they are feeling extremely frustrated because they are not getting enough return on their investment of time, resources and energy spent in an effort to meet the needs of students from diverse cultural backgrounds. The points of this book are to (1) introduce teaching techniques to be used for addressing cultural conflicts that serve to keep us from reaching our goal of dramatically improving student learning, (2) provide practical strategies and considerations for improving the learning of students from diverse backgrounds, and (3) address the topic of increased parental involvement through the use of non-traditional approaches.

There is a level of satisfaction and motivation that one feels as a result of experiencing success. We can certainly relate to this type of feeling when we think about the child that is scared to jump off of the side of a pool into the arms of a trusted adult who is waiting to receive him. In many cases, the child will want to make sure that when he takes the leap in to the pool, someone is actually going to be there to catch him. There is a sense of security that comes as a result of the child following through with his desire, taking the leap, and experiencing success in doing so. The same holds true for teachers. The more that they experience success in terms of improving student learning, the more confident they become in their ability to make the type of difference that will lead to sustainable and measurable results. In other words, success breeds success. If teachers are making gains and feeling positive about their interaction with students, they are likely to put forth effort and maintain the commitment needed to ensure that students achieve socially and academically.

Studies have found a positive relationship between a teacher's sense of self-efficacy and students' classroom achievement. Teachers that believe they can make a difference do make a difference (Educational Research Service 2003). In an effort to increase the likelihood that teachers are confident enough to take a leap on behalf of their students, it is critical that safety nets are established for them. The term "safety net" is used to describe institutional priorities designed to outline expectations and policies needed to ensure that school officials support teachers in reaching the goal of dramatically improving student learning.

I will further address this topic in my next book which describes explicitly the steps that school and district level administrators and Board of Education members should take to support teachers of culturally diverse students. In doing so, these officials will recognize their inherent ability to impact student learning positively.

I have identified several questions that will help us to achieve our objectives for improved student learning. I like to refer to these questions as the "Critical Five."

The Critical Five

1. Why are teachers discovering after tireless work that far too many students are not making recognizable gains in achievement?

2. Does a teacher's background and cultural experiences have a direct impact on his or her delivery of instruction and on assessment of the intellectual capabilities of students whose cultural backgrounds and social experiences are not similar to the teacher's?

3. Which instructional strategies or teaching techniques provide ideal opportunities for teachers to incorporate knowledge of culture into instruction?

4. What approaches can be implemented for increased parental involvement in our elementary and high schools?

5. Are there any non-traditional approaches that we should consider implementing?

Why must we answer these questions?
"An unexamined life is hardly worth living (Socrates)".

Jim Collins, in his book entitled <u>From Good to Great</u>, suggests that we absolutely cannot make a series of good decisions without facing the brutal facts of reality (Collins 2001). If educators are going to make significant progress in educating students from diverse backgrounds we must face the brutal fact that far too many of these students are not reaching their full academic potential. The Critical Five questions that I have posed represent my attempt to address the brutal fact that when compared to their peers, children of color are not making the types of gains in literacy that they are capable of making. If we are going to make significant strides in the right direction, we must face this painful reality. First, to determine the manner in which to proceed, we must make a commitment to engage in conversations that will help us answer the questions posed in the Critical Five. This is the first step toward ensuring the academic success of all students.

The five questions serve as a broad platform for examining the critical factors we must consider. In each of the following chapters, I will pose related questions that will provide a framework for discussion and thoughtful reflection within that chapter and that will help us answer these critical questions and begin to formulate solutions.

In an effort to continuously model the importance of posing and responding to critical questions, at the beginning of each chapter, questions have been identified which provide a framework for discussion and thoughtful reflection.

Chapter One

Knowledge of Self: The Break –Through

"If we don't know our own culture and are uncomfortable with some of our students' backgrounds, we may unintentionally impede their academic development instead of fostering it (Whitaker 2010)."

Questions that drive this chapter of study:

1. How might my cultural background and experiences impact my delivery of instruction, as well as my assessment of student performance?
2. How can I develop healthy interactions with my students in a way that will foster the development of their positive self-identity, thereby increasing the likelihood that they will be successful academically?

A great number of well-intentioned, teachers are at the point of losing faith in one of two things: (1) their ability to make a difference in the lives of their students from diverse backgrounds, or (2) their ability to support their students in making the types of adjustments needed to experience academic and social success in our middle-class organizations called schools. Additionally, teachers fear that their failure to assist students in making adjustments is a hindrance to student achievement and contributes to the upsetting numbers of students that are dropping out of high school.

According to reports provided in 2007 by the National Women's Law Center, nationwide, 37% of Hispanic female students, 40% of African-American female students, and 50% of Native-American/Alaskan-Native female students failed to graduate (National Woman's Law Center 2007). Overall, far too many students are not graduating on time with a regular diploma: low-income and students of color fare the worst in the dropout epidemic. Each year, approximately 1.3 million students fail to graduate from high school: more than half are students of color (Education Week 2010). A student within the age range of sixteen to twenty-four years old who comes from the lowest quartile of family income is about seven times more likely to have dropped out of high school than his or her counterpart who comes from the highest quartile (U.S. Department of Education, National Center for Education Statistics 2010).

The point of this book is to help teachers overcome problems related to a lack of understanding of students' cultural backgrounds and the significant impact that background experiences have on learning. As teachers of students from diverse cultural backgrounds, we can only begin to touch the tip of the iceberg as it relates to increasing student achievement without recognizing that before we can assist students in making a connection to the school they must be able to connect with the teacher. Routman shares with us that the curriculum must first connect with the spirits and the lives of the students. Unless we reach our students' hearts, we have no entry into their minds (Routman 2003).

The two questions posed at the beginning of this chapter, if answered after deep reflection, can serve to provide us with valuable information about how we can better connect with our students and impact student learning in a positive way. In this chapter, I will guide you through the process of reflecting upon and answering these two questions.

Disconnected Students

In my interaction with school-aged children from diverse cultural backgrounds, many of them have indicated that they feel a sense of disconnection from the curriculum and the schooling experience as a whole. Additionally, teachers have indicated that in some instances they feel that there is a sense of disconnection between their culture or background and the background of the students to whom they are providing instruction. I can relate to this sense of feeling disconnected both from the perspectives of a student and that of a teacher.

A high-school-aged student overheard various parts of a presentation that I gave to his teachers. Without being prompted, the student shared that although he loved coming to school every day, he was struggling to gain a sense of positive self-worth. This student further went on to add that the only time he hears mention of a person from his cultural background is when his class is covering a unit on the Civil Rights Movement. Clearly, this student was seeking an opportunity to connect to an image that might inspire him to achieve greatness far beyond even what he could ever imagine.

I would be remiss if I neglected to mention that teachers of all backgrounds have also indicated that in some cases they feel a sense of disconnection between their culture or background experiences and the background of the students that they are instructing. In this chapter I will share personal stories that relate directly to the sense of disconnection experienced by both students and teachers.

This chapter is written to assist you in the process of developing a deeper level of understanding about how your personal experiences impact your delivery of instruction and assessment of what students know and are able to do. In order to accomplish this goal, I have included a framework that I developed for the purpose of guiding educators through a process designed to lead to deeper cultural understandings and awareness of self.

My Search For Relevance

I remember being a school-aged child sitting in class and wondering if my teacher would ever cover concepts that were relevant to my day-to-day experiences and interests. I can vividly recall a time when I was in need of reinforcement that as a child of color it was expected that I would achieve at high academic levels. "Frustrated" is the word that I would use to describe the way that I felt about the fact that far too often I was unable to find (in the curricular materials that I was exposed to) opportunities to connect to successful visions and images of adults or children that looked like me. "Disappointed" is the word that I would use to describe the way that I felt about the fact that there appeared to be no intentional effort on the part of my teachers or administrators (there were no safety nets in place) to validate that I was capable of excellence.

"Confused" is the word that I would use to describe the fact that despite the two points mentioned, deep down inside my soul, I felt that I had the potential to achieve far beyond even what I could imagine. Interestingly enough, my oldest son is currently experiencing a feeling that he, too, has the potential to achieve success academically.

Personal Connection

This was demonstrated via a recent conversation that he initiated with me. While I was in the process of preparing dinner, out of the blue, he said, "Mom, I think that I could be learning more difficult stuff at school." As you can imagine, this comment immediately caught my attention. As a result, I quickly put the preparation of dinner on hold and asked him to elaborate. What came next caught me completely off guard. My son shared that he believed that he could do more in school but felt that he never got to explore topics and concepts that were at a higher level. In an effort to explore how deeply he was thinking I said, "Well, honey, this happens very often in school, what do you propose that teachers do about that?" My son shared that he felt that students should always be given the opportunity to "do harder work." Furthermore, he added, "If I am never given an opportunity to try it, how will my teacher ever know if I can really do it or not?" In other words, my son was struggling internally. Throughout his personal life, he has been able to watch members of his family excel both professionally and personally. He has also had the benefit of seeing first-hand the type of hard work that it takes for a person to achieve his or her dreams. In essence, I believe that my son has begun to internalize his personal experiences and then associate them with the potential to achieve greatness academically. He is conflicted when he believes that the bar has been set too low for him and as a result, he feels a sense of disconnection from the curriculum and the schooling experience as a whole. When I reflect on this insightful conversation that I had with my elementary-aged son, I am reminded of the saying "Students do not rise to low expectations." Unfortunately in many classrooms and homes across the country, our children/students are not articulating this feeling of frustration. More often than not, the result of this feeling is played out in the form of misbehavior.

As mentioned earlier, while serving in the capacity of school administrator one afternoon, I received notice from one of my teachers that a male student was consistently disruptive throughout an entire school day. After hearing the frustration in the voice of the teacher, I asked that the student be escorted to the office where he was to remain until I completed a meeting with a group of teachers. During the middle of the meeting, I rushed in to my office to obtain some additional materials and noticed right away that the student had gotten out of the seat that he was assigned to and was engaged in a conversation with the secretary. Without hesitation I informed the student that he should report back to the assigned seat until further notice. Later, after I returned to the main office, the secretary asked if I would be interested in hearing what the student asked her.

I am not sure if I was more curious or anxious to know what he could have been discussing with her. After all, he did spend half of the school day disrupting the class and frustrating one of my best teachers. All of a sudden, the secretary hit me with some information that would change the way that I view the importance of the work that we do as educators. She informed me that the student asked, "Is there anybody in this school that can teach me how to read?" Without warning, tears rolled down my face and I began to feel that a heavy burden had been placed on my back as a school leader. Weighted down by the feeling of helplessness, I responded by using the Public Announcement System to ask that any teacher in the building that was not working with a student at the time "Please meet me in the lounge." I shared with the teachers that although we are all working very hard to increase student achievement, we have a student that has just verbally expressed a desire to learn how to read. It appears that we have missed something along the way.

Fortunately, the student felt a strong enough connection to the building secretary that he was comfortable enough to share his very relevant feelings. I explained to the teachers that it was my belief that the negative behavior displayed by the student was an outward demonstration of the frustration that he feels as a result of not knowing how to read. As a team we began the process of developing a more comprehensive plan of action for addressing his needs.

Author's First-Hand Experience

Coincidentally, I can relate to the feeling of disconnection articulated by classroom teachers as I reflect on the fact that I am an African-American woman and that I spent a great deal of my childhood living on military bases protected by the affection of loving parents and the security of the military police who manned the entrance of the Air Force Bases on which we lived. However, when I first began my teaching career in Atlanta, there was a cultural conflict between my background experiences and the backgrounds of the very students that looked like me. This disconnection manifested itself in several ways. My siblings and I grew up in a very structured environment. Therefore, as a classroom teacher, I had a pre-conceived vision of how my students were to behave and demonstrate what they know. For example I can vividly recall a time in which I posed a question during a literacy lesson.

As opposed to raising their hands and waiting to be called upon, my students began to blurt out their answers. There were so many students talking at one time that I could not make out what any of them were saying. After several days of this consistent response from students, I realized that because of the their style of responding to my questions, there were times in which I believe that I failed to gain an accurate level of understanding regarding what my students knew and were able to do. I made the mistake of focusing on the fact that they appeared to be disruptive and now believe that my focus should have been more on developing a more thorough level of understanding of the various ways in which my students preferred to demonstrate what they knew and were able to do.

I will elaborate more on the need to engage in this thought process later in the final chapter of this book. I was equally puzzled by my students' use of comfortable language throughout the regular school day. I now believe that I made the mistake of not assisting students in the process of making a connection between their comfortable language and the academic language needed to experience success in our middle-class organizations called schools. Many of us experience this similar conflict when interacting with our bilingual students.

We often find ourselves trying to figure out when and where it is best to afford our students the opportunity to speak in their native language or use a communication style with which they are most comfortable. The reality is that most of our vocabulary comes directly from our own personal experiences. Therefore it is important that teachers validate the use of the natural language that our students demonstrate in the classroom setting. Our goal, in essence, is to aid students in connecting their natural verbal expressions to the academic language used in the school setting. In an effort to provide a clearer picture of what this disconnection might feel like to the students, I would like to share the following: Several years ago I experienced a cultural disconnection related to the use of language while visiting an appliance store along with my husband.

Prior to arriving at the store I called to provide details regarding the purchase that I wanted to make. After being greeted by the sales associate that I spoke with on the phone, she indicated that she wanted to talk with me about a wide variety of ranges. She explained that they had several different colors and styles that I could choose from. After about ten minutes into the conversation, I began to experience some of the internal stress that students feel when we have completed a lesson and a few of them come to the realization that they failed to grasp the most important concepts introduced at the very beginning of the lesson. When the associate walked away for a brief moment, I began to explain to my husband that I had no idea what a range was. He stated, "Well, I guess we better find out what it is, if she wants us to spend money on it." Finally, I built up enough courage to share with the associate that I was in need of a stove and not a range. It was at that moment that I learned that *range* is a term that is sometimes used to describe a stove. This is however, a term to which I had never been exposed. I immediately connected this experience to the types of cultural conflicts that are taking place in America's classrooms.

In a classroom setting, the culturally-responsive teacher might validate the student by stating that the use of the term "stove" is accurate, however, the author of the story that we are currently reading has decided to use the term "range." A follow-up to the discussion could be to ask the students in the class to find out if their parent or guardian refers to the appliance mentioned as a stove or a range. Doing so validates the students' use of vocabulary, provides him or her with the opportunity to connect it to the use of the school language and then makes the home-school connection.

Another cultural conflict that I experienced during my first year of teaching was related to the amount of dancing that took place in my classroom. My friends find this quite interesting because every time I hear one of my favorite songs I start dancing. Trust me, I really do. Yet, I have always felt that there was a time and a place for everything. However, my students taught me the importance of being creative and expanding my thinking. They loved to dance and they took the opportunity to express themselves in the form of movement every time that they had a free moment to spare. My students taught me to appreciate who they were. In the community in which they lived, they spent fun evenings dancing to the greatest musical hits by their favorite artists. It became my responsibility to figure out how to help students channel their positive energy in a way that would benefit them academically. Without any knowledge of the fact that I was demonstrating culturally-responsive teaching behaviors, I found myself providing my students with the opportunity to move around as much as possible. I even began the process of playing soft music as they entered the classroom each morning. I introduced them to jazz and classical music. I then asked them to compare some of the sounds that they heard in the music that I selected to the sounds and beats that they danced to while enjoying time with their family. I expressed a genuine appreciation for their family traditions. On a few occasions, the students began to initiate conversations regarding the likenesses and differences between the types of music that they liked to dance to and the types of music that I preferred. As a result we established a bond that I could build upon while challenging them academically.

Cultural conflicts in the classroom are, in many cases, the result of differences in the personal, academic, ethnic and economic experiences (both positive and negative) of teachers and students throughout their lives (Whitaker 2010). These experiences shape our thinking about the world. They also shape our beliefs about the manner in which we should think and express ourselves. Once we gain the confidence needed to engage in the process of developing a deeper understanding of how cultural experiences play a significant role in our interactions with students, many cultural conflicts can be successfully addressed.

Provided is a framework I developed in my published DVD entitled "The Culturally-Responsive Teacher: How

Understanding Culture Positively Impacts Instruction and Student Achievement" (Whitaker 2010). This tool was developed for the purpose of guiding educators through a process designed to lead to deeper cultural understanding and awareness of self. During workshop presentations, I use this process to encourage adults to self-disclose to their peers pertinent information about their individual culture:

Discover Your Culture Framework

Family life	In a small group setting, participants are asked to share details regarding the community that they lived in as child, and also indicate whether or not they have had regular interactions with cultures other than their own throughout child and adulthood.
Economic-class structure	Participants are then asked to self-disclose information about which economic-class structure they are most able to relate to based on their childhood experiences.
Ethnic background	The next step in the process is

	for participants to share information about their family traditions, special gatherings and holiday celebrations.
Academic preparation	In this phase of the process, participants are asked to describe their experiences as a student in school, as well as information related to their academic experiences after high school.

Figure 1.1

The benefits of engaging in a process of this nature as reported by teachers has been that it allowed them to gain an elevated level of knowledge of cultures other than their own and a better understanding of how life experiences impact their interaction with their peers and students. In essence, they gained a more in-depth level of understanding of the "lenses" by which they and others view the world. Additionally, upon the completion of engaging in this process, teachers are asked to discuss how the experiences that they shared using the framework might impact their delivery of instruction and interaction with students. I would like to suggest that, as teachers, we must take time regularly to consider our responses to this question in particular.

In order to model the process I will share the following information regarding my cultural background as it relates to the framework described in figure 1.1.

Family Life

I am the oldest of three children. My experiences are unique in that, as the daughter of a father in the Air Force, I spent a significant portion of my life traveling across the country. As a very young child, my family spent time in Japan, and by the time I graduated from high school (in Anchorage, Alaska), we had lived in as many as five different states. I attribute much of my present success with maneuvering in settings in which people from a wide variety of cultural backgrounds are interacting to the experiences that I had traveling as a child. In several of the states in which I lived, my family and I lived on the military base, so to some degree, one might say that I was sheltered from some of the day-to-day happenings of life outside of the military setting.

Economic-Class Structure and Family Background

With regards to my family's economic status, because of my father's affiliation with the military, our family was afforded the comfort of a steady paycheck and the luxury of the health benefits that far too many Americans are struggling to be able to afford in our current economy. Although my immediate family members and I did a great deal of moving, we held on to our southern roots and as much as possible, the rock of our home, my beautiful mother, maintained our family tradition of cooking entirely too much food for each and every party that we ever had. Much like one might see in movies depicting the traditions of African-American families, it is true that in the Robinson (my maiden name) family, cooking was from the heart. My mother has always poured her heart and soul into her southern cooking and always preferred to cook without company. She still requests to be left alone to "do what she does" in the kitchen until the meal is prepared. I guess that is why as a wife and mother of two, I still have not prepared a Thanksgiving meal of my own.

Academic Preparation

My academic preparation is a part of what drives me to do the work that I have committed to spending the rest of my life doing. I currently hold the Degree of Doctor of Education in Educational Leadership and Administration. In August of 2003, I completed several years of study and successfully earned the Educational Specialist Degree as well as the Superintendent's endorsement and I currently maintain Superintendent certification in the states of Illinois and Georgia. Additionally I hold a Master of Arts Degree and Bachelor of Arts Degree in Education. When interacting with educators across the country, my peers are tremendously supportive and very often begin to share information regarding how they would like to leverage themselves so they are able to experience the success that appears to have come almost flawlessly for me. I now find myself sharing with audiences that "you may see me in my glory moment at the time, but it is most important that you understand my story."

My Story

When I reflect on the academic success that I have experienced as an undergraduate and graduate student over the last decade it makes it even more difficult to believe that I have actually made it. The painful truth is that as a young student, I struggled to demonstrate my knowledge on standardized achievement tests. As a result, I developed a phobia. I can still remember being near the age of ten and being confused as to why my teacher did not realize that I had a gift of articulating what I was thinking. I like to think that it is that gift that has attributed to the success that I feel while delivering a keynote speech, or professional development workshop. When I was in elementary school, I often had fill-in-the-blank sheets in which students were to fill in the answers to questions that were posed on a reading exam. The issue that I faced almost on a daily basis was this: if I was given the opportunity to demonstrate what I knew by articulating my thoughts orally in a public setting, my teachers would automatically gain a positive sense of what I knew.

Conversely, each and every time that I was asked to demonstrate my knowledge base by participating in a fill-in-the-blank test or performing on a standardized test, I would literally freeze up and my mind would go blank. I felt trapped and unable to articulate the level of frustration that I was feeling. After all, I was taught to believe the teacher was always right. If I was assigned a particular assessment tool to be used to evaluate my intellectual capabilities, I wanted to believe that at some point the assessment tool was being selected with me in mind. Unfortunately, too often this was not the case. As a result of my low performance on standardized tests, my teachers questioned my intellectual capabilities and my fear of taking standardized tests was never addressed. This issue resurfaced itself throughout both my junior high and high school academic careers. As opposed to having access to the "harder stuff" as my son so eloquently describes it, I believe that my exposure to on-grade-level or above-grade-level material was minimal at best. Because of the mismatch between the assessment measures used to determine my knowledge base and my preferred method of demonstrating what I know, my teachers were at a disadvantage. As a result, many of them were unable to build upon my strengths. They never tapped in to my giftedness or my strengths as an intellectual being.

While speaking with teachers and administrators across the country, I have learned that more often than not, others have had similar experiences. I have also found that many adults become ashamed and embarrassed while self-disclosing details regarding their academic experiences. I have found that most of us tend to want to put it in the back of our minds and pretend as if it never happened. I, however, deem it necessary to engage in thoughtful reflection about my experiences so that history does not repeat itself. It is my personal experiences that have helped to make me a better teacher and administrator. I must admit I never would have thought that I would now have the courage
to share these experiences in the form of writing.

The Lowest Point

This lack of having a solid academic foundation smacked me right in the face just before I graduated with my first degree in education. Much like one might feel after having had a bad dream, in the next part of my story, this issue played out for me in the most horrific way as I prepared to graduate from college and receive my first degree in Education. This part of my story represents one of the lowest points in my entire life. In the spring of 1994, while preparing to graduate with my very first college degree, I was delivered the news (via U.S. Mail) that I failed to pass the Georgia Teacher Certification Test. I was completely devastated and can remember experiencing depression in a way that is too painful to describe. Ironically, while in college, I was described by the professors in the Education Department as one of the students that would become one of the best in the field of education.

I remember trying to figure out how I was going to tell all of my professors that after all of the years and the time that they had invested in me, I failed them, I failed myself, I failed my parents. I carried a heavy burden on my shoulders. It was my faith in someone much more powerful than me that allowed me to hold my head up just long enough to make it across the stage to receive the degree of Bachelor of Arts in Early Childhood Education. While my peers went off to celebrate the occasion, as you can imagine, thoughts ran through my mind at a rapid pace. I began to think about how quickly I could retake the teacher certification test in hopes that I would pass the exam in enough time to join the ranks of my peers that were fortunate enough to pass the exam the first time. This period of time was particularly difficult because, I had been offered at least two teaching positions but was unable to take either of them because of my inability to demonstrate my intellectual capabilities on one standardized assessment measure.

This experience crippled my spirits and caused me to question my own strengths as a teacher candidate. I began to ask questions of myself that were specific to whether or not I was worthy of becoming an educator. In an attempt to keep the faith and work hard to achieve my dream of becoming one the best in my field of study, I set out to take the Georgia teacher certification test once again and once again, I failed to pass the exam. In fact, I had to take the test several other times before finally passing the exam nearly three weeks after the start of the school year in which I had hoped to have my own classroom. Eventually I passed the examination, as is evidenced by my current level of professional experiences. Since then, I have successfully passed state level exams in the state of Illinois at the principal and superintendent level. I am forever grateful for the faith that kept me grounded during such an incredibly difficult time. And isn't it amazing how things have a tendency to work out on our behalf?

My perseverance took me from struggling to pass the test needed to certify me at the classroom level and less than fifteen years later I passed the Superintendent's examination, which certified me to hold the highest possible position in America's public school setting. It is important for us to recognize that not all of our students have the faith or support systems in place that we have. As a result, when the going gets tough, they may have a more difficult time persevering. Our role becomes more important because we may unknowingly be one of the very few adults that make up the system of support for our students. As has been evidenced, this is a role that we cannot take lightly.

As a student at every level possible (from elementary school to the doctoral level in graduate school), I have had both extremely high moments and very low moments. I have had the opportunity to travel the country and experience opportunities that some, but not all, of my students have had the opportunity to experience. It is of the utmost importance to me that I continue to reflect on how my personal, academic and professional experiences shape my view of the world and contribute to any cultural conflicts that may have taken place in my classroom. It is this deep type of self-reflection that allows teachers to experience the "break-through" necessary to connect with their students. As we continue to reflect upon how our experiences have shaped our worldview, we must stop to consider how we can develop healthy interactions with our students in a way that will foster the development of their positive self-identity thereby increasing the likelihood that they will be successfully academically?

Developing healthy interactions with our students begins with teachers and administrators making a decision to familiarize themselves with the cultures and backgrounds of their students. While making this point with a group of teachers in Los Angeles, California, I was posed with a question regarding whether or not I was suggesting that teachers should be required to obtain advanced degrees focused on culture. My response to a question of this nature is as follows: Every teacher has to enter into this process at whatever level he or she is most comfortable. Many teachers have elected to obtain English as a Second Language Endorsements so that they can better communicate and interact with their bilingual students. Other teachers have worked with their peers to engage in non-traditional practices for the purposes of learning about the culture of the students in their classrooms.

Non-Traditional Approach for Increased Parental Involvement

To further elaborate on this point, while conducting a workshop presentation in Peoria, Illinois, I learned that an entire teaching and administrative staff made a commitment to learn more about the families of the students that they were serving. Therefore, at the beginning of the school year, as opposed to hosting the traditional parent/teacher conference, this school decided to try something different. The staff at this school wanted different results and was prepared to do something different in order to achieve their goal. At the beginning of the school year, they conducted a non-traditional parent/teacher conference. The staff invited the parents and guardians of the students to lead the conference by sharing information (in the most creative way they would like) about their culture and family traditions. The teachers shared with me that the event was a huge success. Many of them indicated that they were able to relate to students much better after learning more about their families. As a result, they were better able to assist their students in making a connection between content material and their background experiences.

One teacher shared that the grandmother of one of her students actually had her grandson bring in a rocking chair that had been passed down from generation to generation. During the parent-teacher conference, the grandmother wrapped herself in a traditional head wrap and read one of her favorite folk tales to her grandson and the teacher. Several of the teachers indicated that they had more parental involvement during the school year that the non-traditional parent/teacher conference was held then they had in a three-to-five-year time span. They attributed the increase in involvement to the fact that they made a deliberate attempt to learn more about their students' family traditions and cultural backgrounds. As a result, the parents and guardians of the students felt more of a connection to the school and to the teachers.

It is important to develop a deep sense of connection to your students so that you are better equipped to address cultural conflicts that may take place during instruction. During a conversation with a teacher in the northwest suburbs of Illinois, he shared that he was deeply saddened by an event that took place in his classroom. This teacher was conducting a lesson focused on the topic of the Montgomery Boycott. In an effort to ensure that his students were involved in the lesson, he asked the students to share, from their perspectives, what it might have been like to be a part of the boycott. Many of the students were eager to engage in the conversation. However after about ten minutes into the lesson the teacher noticed that one of the students in his classroom had his head down on his desk. The student put a finger in each ear in an attempt to drown out the sound of his peers talking. While talking with me, the teacher indicated that he was unsure as to whether or not he should approach the student. He also shared that he decided that because he cares about all of this students, he should approach him but did not know what to say. He added that he felt helpless and could not think of anyone that he could call that would be prepared to assist him address such a sensitive topic. Somehow he built up enough courage to ask the student to share his feelings with him.

The student indicated that the Montgomery Bus Boycott represented a very painful time in history that he would prefer to forget. I will never forget the look in this male teacher's eyes when he had this conversation with me. With tears running down his face, he said, "I tried, Dr. Whitaker." "I tried to bring in to the lesson something that I knew that my African-American students could relate to but I blew it." He asked what should he have done and how should he have handled the situation. I began by applauding the teacher's commitment to engaging all of his students in the learning process. Furthermore, I advised the teacher that in cases in which he feels that he might address a topic that is sensitive in nature he should consider exploring the topic (along with the students) from dual perspectives. For example, the students could have all been given an opportunity to discuss the meaning of the term "bystander". A bystander as described by Webster's dictionary is one present but not taking part in a situation or event. The teacher could have shared with students that in difficult situations, we have a choice regarding how we want to respond. We can choose to serve as bystanders or we could choose to stand up for the rights of others.

A lesson of this nature could have ultimately resulted in the teacher empowering the students by giving them an opportunity to discuss instances in which they have chosen to serve as a bystander and instances in which they have elected to stand up for the rights of others. It is with this frame of mind that the teacher could have provided focus for the lesson. By doing so, the student in question may have felt that he had been given an opportunity to work with his peers to determine the most appropriate way to deal with his feeling of pain. A lesson of this nature could provide students with a skill that can be used throughout life.

In another situation, a teacher shared with me that she was concerned about the fact that her students of color did not have enough positive interactions with adults from similar cultural backgrounds. She further went on to add that she was unsure as to how much of a role that she should play in terms of making sure that this need was met for her students. I shared with the teacher that it is critically important that teachers make an intentional effort to assist their students in developing positive self-identities. Our goal is also to ensure that all of our students are able to see themselves as intelligent individuals capable of making significant contributions to society. Many schools are making an attempt to achieve this goal without ever exposing children of color to images of successful people that look like them.

Many teachers across America take the opportunity to invite adult professionals to visit their schools. I am suggesting that we should expand our search for interested professionals to include adults from the ethnic and cultural backgrounds of the students that are represented in our classrooms and schools. The brutal fact of reality is that our teachers are not provided enough opportunities to address topics of this nature in a safe environment that is committed to developing their cultural competencies. As a result, well-intentioned teachers are left alone to make decisions about the most appropriate manner in which to discuss or address a topic or issue that they too may be uncomfortable with addressing.

Teachers must commit to engaging in deep reflection on a regular basis in order to experience the paradigm shift in thinking needed to respond proactively to the cultural conflicts that are taking place in America's classrooms.

Chapter Two

Resolving Cultural Conflicts:

Possessing the Will to Respond

"There are cultural conflicts taking place in classrooms across the entire country. Teachers need a safe place to talk so that they can be about the business of dramatically increasing student achievement (Whitaker 2010)."

Questions that drive this chapter of study:

1. What opportunities am I providing for students to develop an appreciation of the cultures that are represented in our classrooms?
2. How confident am I in my ability to identify and successfully address the cultural conflicts that are taking place in my classroom or school?

As teachers are going through the process of determining the impact of their cultural experiences on their delivery of instruction and assessment of student learning, it becomes equally important for them to engage the students in the process of reflecting as well. As early as kindergarten, students begin to develop perceptions about who they are as individuals. By the time young students reach adolescence this sense of being able to connect and identify with the world around them is a process explored by all students regardless of their ethnic or cultural background. This sense of questioning one's place in society is played out in many different ways. For example, very often as boys begin to mature they may become more aggressive in their interaction with their peers in an effort to demonstrate their masculinity. African-American students (both male and female) may go through a process of exploring racial identity. This process is described by author W.E. Cross as the immersion/emersion stage and is explained as a process in which the students make a conscious effort to learn more about one's culture with the support of peers from the same race (Cross, W.E., 1991).

The question becomes a matter of how these differences or processes of exploration are played out in the form of student interaction and behavior on a daily basis. Classrooms provide an opportunity for students to be exposed to cultures, styles of communication and verbal expression different from their own. Due to the fact that many of our neighborhoods still remain very segregated places, it becomes even more important that teachers take advantage of the opportunity to ensure that our students develop the cultural competencies needed to interact effectively with others. I can certainly relate to this need as I am reminded of my interaction with a young white female student who shared with me that she was thrilled to learn that I would be her administrator. After inquiring about why she felt this way, she indicated that she felt that it was important for the other African-American students to see me and to know that they too could be successful.

In my own moment of quiet reflection, I could not help but think about how beneficial it was for all of my students, White, Black, Hispanic and Asian, to have an opportunity to *see* me but more importantly, to get to know me. I then began to imagine what a serious disadvantage for my students it would be if they went throughout their entire childhood (and in far too many cases, adulthood) without ever having an opportunity to interact with an adult outside of their own culture. I am even more concerned about the lack of exposure when I think about how fast our world is changing in terms of demographic diversity. Demographic shifts are bringing schools more diverse populations. Educators are striving to respond but many lack the cultural proficiency to address the needs of a diverse student population (Nelson and Guerra 2007).

Most educational leaders are aware that their districts have a gap in achievement among racial, ethnic, and socio-economic groups of students, but are unaware that the problem goes beyond achievement test scores. Most importantly, they may not understand what steps to take to address the issue (Nelson and

Guerra 2007). This book has been written for the purpose of providing teachers and administrators with explicit details for how to develop the cultural competencies of the adults and students in our schools.

Is it possible, that without multiple levels of exposure to adults outside of their own culture, my innocent students could have developed a very narrow sense of reality? By multiple levels, I am referring to the need for all students to see positive images of many people from a wide variety of cultures serving in the capacity of their classroom teachers and educational administrators. It is also important for students to see people like themselves in textbooks. Unfortunately, there is a scarcity of educational materials that give realistic representations of the experiences of people of color.

Cooperative Learning in A Culturally-Responsive Learning Environment

Much research has been done in the area of cooperative learning. Educators across the country are making attempts to provide students with opportunities to engage in assignments that are geared toward promoting group interaction and collective problem-solving. Processes of this nature would prove much more effective within the context of teaching children how important it is to rid themselves of a natural human desire to engage in group-think. By hearing the thoughts of peers from outside their cultural group, they open themselves up to receiving a wider variety of perspectives which can lead to them making an informed decision about how to proceed with meeting the objectives of their lessons.

In the workforce, these types of adult interactions can very well lead to higher productivity and an improved bottom line. Having said that, I cannot help but ask where we expect students to learn these critical skills, if we are not intentionally providing them with a platform by which to develop their social interaction skills and abilities. Teachers have shared with me quite frankly, that they do not know the most effective manner in which to engage students in the process of discussing cultural differences. Perhaps this is the case because many of us were not given the opportunity to do so when we were school-aged. In order to create the type of environment in which students are working toward developing their cultural competencies, teachers should begin the school year by using the framework that I have developed in figure 1.2.

This framework has been developed in response to this need. You will recognize that this student framework (figure 1.2) is similar to the framework provided in figure 1.1 for teacher reflection on their own experiences.

Being culturally competent means possessing the commitment, the confidence, and the skills needed to engage in deep conversations about cultural conflicts (Whitaker 2010). I have provided a framework and related scenarios that we can use to support students in developing their cultural competencies.

Student Culture Framework

Your Family	Students are asked to share information that they feel great about sharing related to their family (suggestions may be the number of siblings in the home, favorite aunts, uncles, cousins or pets). The students may want to bring in artifacts, pictures etc. which provide their peers with an even better view of their world.
Favorite things to do	During this step in the process the students are asked to share information related to their favorite things to do with their family and friends.
Learning experiences	Students are asked to share information related to their favorite subjects in school. They should identify what they

	consider to be their strengths and weaknesses as well as individual learning goals that they have or plan to establish.
Uniqueness	In the final step in the process, the students are asked to discuss, with at least two-to-three peers, information related to what makes them alike and what makes them different.

Figure 1.2

Depending upon the grade level of the students, teachers are encouraged to implement a modified version of the framework. The final step in this process is for teachers to pose the following guiding questions for each student to respond to both orally and in writing wherever appropriate:

1. How did you feel about sharing information about yourself to another classmate or peer?

2. What did you learn about your classmate or peer that you did not know?

3. In what ways are you like your classmates? In what ways are you different?

4. Enrichment question: In what ways do your life experiences shape the way that you interact with your classmates or others?

In an effort to further support teachers in developing their students' cultural competencies, I have identified the following scenarios as premier examples of opportunities to discuss cultural dynamics with students. It is important to recognize that culturally- responsive teachers are constantly on the "look-out" for teachable moments much like the examples that are provided here. The scenarios are derived from examples of cultural conflicts that have been shared with me by classroom teachers as I have traveled the country with a sharp focus on this topic.

****

Cultural Conflict Scenarios

****

Scenario One:

A female primary-aged-student approaches the classroom teacher and indicates that she is extremely upset because of a negative interaction that she has had with the Native-American girls in her classroom. The teacher inquires about what has caused her to be upset and the student shares that the other girls are always together and she feels that she is not provided with an opportunity to bond with them.

The student further goes on to explain that she really wants to get to know the other girls but they seem to be uninterested in forming a friendship. As a result, she feels isolated and is concerned that it will somehow affect her ability to concentrate on her studies.

In this situation, the culturally-responsive teacher elects to address the problem head-on. Because she has developed a sense of self-awareness and possesses the confidence needed to address the issue, the teacher makes a decision to engage the students in a conversation about what appears to be a cultural conflict between the girls. The classroom teacher brings all of the students together and informs the Native-American students that their peer is interested in forming a bond with them but feels left out. The teacher then goes on to ask the students to share information about how their friendship was formed and what makes them close.

The students shared that they all live in the same neighborhood and their parents are very close. They further went on to inform the teacher that their families are all involved in a similar community-service project two weekends out of every month. After their volunteer work is done during the weekends, their families make it a habit to get together to go for lunch. Essentially, the girls indicated that it was the time that they spent together outside of the regular school day that contributed to the sense of closeness that they felt to one another.

Reflection Session:

****

What is your response?
Please take a moment to discuss with your peer and reflect on how you propose that this situation be resolved.
****

The culturally-responsive teacher provided the following interpretation of the girls' explanation:

Teacher*: So what I hear you saying is that you have formed a friendship that goes beyond the walls of our school or classroom.*

Group of Girls*: Yes, we get to spend a lot of time together at home and at school and because of that we trust and feel close to one another.*

Teacher*: What can we do to make sure that we are responsive to your classmate's desire to develop a close friendship with each of you?*

Group of Girls*: We can approach her at school and make sure that she is included as opposed to excluding her during our social interactions. We will make an effort to make sure that she feels welcomed to join us at any time.*

Individual Student*: I was completely unaware that my peers were spending additional time together outside of the school day. I now have a better understanding of why they were more likely to be very protective of the bond that they had formed. I no longer feel that there was a deliberate attempt to exclude me but, instead, I believe that my peers are more familiar with one another and enjoy the friendship that they have formed. I am anxious to develop a similar bond with each of them.*

****

Reflection Session

****

1. *What were the benefits of this open level of communication to the student that expressed her concern about being left out of the group?*
2. *What were the benefits of this conversation to her peers that were involved in the conversation?*
3. *What are your thoughts about how the teacher elected to handle the situation?*
4. *Would you have responded differently and, if so, how?*

****

Scenario Two:

A group of English-speaking male students report to the classroom teacher that they are angry about the fact that students whose native language is not English always prefer to speak in their native language during transitions from one class period to another. The English-only speaking students indicated that they felt that the actions of their peers were rude and inconsiderate. They further added that they often feel completely excluded from conversations that were taking place in a language that they could not speak or understand. The students insisted that the students should be required to speak only in English while in school.

****

Reflection Session:

Please take a moment to reflect on how you would respond to a situation of this nature.

****

The culturally-responsive teacher responded as follows:
Teacher: I would like to discuss your interaction with one another during our transition period. It is my understanding that

several of you prefer to communicate using your native language throughout the day. Your peers have indicated that they are very upset when this occurs mainly because they feel excluded from the conversations and are unsure as to whether or not you are sharing information that should be of concern or interest to them.

Students: *We prefer to speak in our native language because it is the way in which we best communicate what we are thinking. When we are in class we feel that we have to work overtime to generate our thoughts and then translate what we are thinking into words that may not be natural for us to use. Using our native language during this time provides us with a break from working so hard to say the right things or use the correct phrases. It is our opportunity to be free to just say what we are thinking in the way that we are most comfortable with doing so. We love it and it keeps us from feeling so stressed.*

Students that issued the complaint: *Wow! We were completely unaware of the fact that our peers felt so much pressure about articulating their thoughts using English. We did however want them to understand how we felt when they were doing so. We felt completely uncomfortable because we were unable to develop a sense of what they were discussing. This left us with a very uneasy feeling about the intent of the conversation. We still* *believe that they should not be speaking in their native language while in school. It just makes us too uncomfortable.*

Teacher addresses the students whom the complaint was filed against*: It is important for each of you to recognize that our goal is to create a culturally-responsive environment. By doing so, we must maintain our commitment to being inclusive rather than exclusive. Therefore, I am going to suggest that in the event that your peers express a genuine interest to be included in conversations, I would like to encourage you to include your peers in your discussions. Please know that this is not a requirement, however it is in direct alignment with our collective decision to develop culturally-responsive relationships. In the event that you question the intent of the peers that ask to be a part of your conversations, you are asked to involve me immediately. My role will be to assist each of you in working through any misunderstandings that may be occurring as a result of your interaction with one another.*

****

Reflection Session:

****

1. *What were the benefits of a conversation of this nature to the students that filed the initial complaint?*

2. *What were the benefits of this conversation to the students that were communicating using their native language?*

3. *What are your thoughts about how the teacher elected to handle this situation?*

4. *Would you have responded differently, if so how?*

xxxxxxxxxxxxxxxxxxxxxxxxxxxxxxxxxxxxxxxxxxxxxx

Scenario Three:

In a high school setting, students complain to their teacher "There is a group of Black kids grouped together in the cafeteria." They further explain that this appears to be a reoccurring habit. Every day they enter the school cafeteria (particularly during lunch) they notice that a great number of the African-American students are always sitting together. They add that this type of behavior causes them to believe that their peers are "up to something." They seek out the teacher's advice in an effort to determine whether or not they should be concerned about the groups' intentions.

****

Reflection Session:

Please take a moment to indicate how you would respond to a situation of this nature.

****

The teacher is completely comfortable with addressing this situation after having participated in a group discussion initiated by the African-American students several weeks before this incident. During the conversation, the students shared that they feel a tremendous amount of stress as a result of having to conform to certain styles of behavior or expression of thought that are not, as they describe, always in alignment with the ways in which they naturally express themselves or demonstrate what they know. The students added that they feel that being together in the cafeteria provides them with a much-needed opportunity to relieve the stress that they feel upon entering the doors of the school each day. Very often they use the time period to provide informal support to one another as they go through the process of developing a positive self-identity.

Note: The students' explanation is in alignment with author Beverly Tatum's perspective that the developmental need to explore the meaning of one's identity with others who are engaged in a similar process manifests itself informally in school corridors and cafeterias across the country (Tatum 2007). Black youth benefit from seeking support from those who have had similar experiences (Tatum 2007).

After careful consideration, the teacher decided to bring the students together to engage in an open and honest dialogue about their feelings.

Teacher speaks to the group of students that shared their concern: *You have spoken with me extensively about how you feel about the African -American students sitting together in the cafeteria. Please tell your peers how you feel.*

Students that launched the complaint: *Well, we are not really trying to get them in trouble we just want to feel comfortable when we walk in the cafeteria. When we walk in and see them all together like that it makes us concerned about what they might be discussing or doing.*

African-American students: *We find it terribly disturbing that you are concerned when you see us sitting together. We don't get that feeling when we see other groups of kids within the same culture sitting together. We now feel as if it is ok for other cultures to formulate bonds but it is not ok for us to do the same.*
Students that launched the complaint: *We never thought about it like that. We spend time together in the cafeteria everyday and no*

one ever questions why we are together. I guess we have never really taken the time to explore why we might feel threatened when we see you all in a group together.

African-American students*: We understand one another. Therefore, we look forward to being together at certain times during the day so we can just be ourselves. It is sometimes the only time that we have to relieve frustration that we have as a result of our history, our culture and our lives being left out of curricular materials. If that isn't enough to be concerned about, we are also very much aware of the fact that we are completely absent from having a place in the district-initiated gifted education or magnet programs.*

Teacher*: It has become crystal clear to me that we must continue to make opportunities to have these conversations in our classroom regularly. It is one thing to say that our goal is to create a culturally responsive learning environment. It is another thing, however, to actually commit to a specific process for doing so. I would like each of you to assist me in developing a plan of action for addressing issues of this nature on an on-going basis. Our goal would be to grow to be able to respond to matters like this proactively as opposed to reactively.*

As a result of their conversations with one another and the teacher, both groups of students began to recognize how their behavior negatively impacted their peers. After hearing the African-American students describe their reasons for sitting together in the cafeteria, their peers developed a genuine desire to learn more about how they might form a peer group designed to encourage communication of this nature on an on-going basis. The African-American students indicated that they were unaware as to how their peers were feeling about their lunchtime chats. They also agreed that on-going conversation was important.

****

Reflection Session:

1. *Please take a moment to discuss how you would foster on-going communication on this topic with the students involved in this situation.*
2. *How would you evaluate the effectiveness of your plan of action?*
3. *What would be the benefits to all students involved?*

In summary, our goal as educators is to ensure that all of our students are interacting with one another in a positive manner and to address (with confidence) any conflicts that may arise as a result of cultural misunderstandings on a case-by-case basis. In culturally- responsive schools, all students are seen as having inherent resources and ability to experience academic success. It becomes the school's responsibility to ensure that avoidable cultural conflicts do not thwart that inherent potential for learning (Educational Research Service 2003). The point of this chapter is to reemphasize the importance of creating a classroom environment that acknowledges the fact that cultural conflicts will arise and to establish a culture that is committed to working through them.

Chapter Three

The Move From Knowing To Doing: What Can I Do Tomorrow?

"To know and not to do is really not to know at all (Covey)."

Question that drives this chapter of study:

> 1. Which instructional strategies or teaching techniques provide ideal opportunities for teachers to incorporate knowledge of culture into instruction?

In this chapter we will review instructional strategies for improving the learning of students from diverse backgrounds. These strategies can be implemented in your classroom as early as tomorrow.

A middle-school teacher gave what appeared to be an assignment that would involve students thinking about history. She asked each of them to pretend that he or she was alive during the U.S. Civil War and write a letter to someone who was also alive at that time. The student was very distraught about the assignment and expressed concern to his mother. He explained to her that he was unclear as to how he was to go about completing this assignment, which made him uncomfortable and presented some difficulties with figuring out what to write. While speaking with his mother, he posed questions such as, "If I were a slave, would I be able to read and write?" Am I supposed to pretend as if I was White (Garcia and Willis 2001)?" The thoughts of this student represent the experiences that children from diverse backgrounds and their teachers have stated are occurring in classrooms across our country on a regular basis. Because this story represents reoccurring incidents familiar to all of us, it is imperative that we determine whether or not we are adequately prepared to address cultural conflicts related to our students' curricular experiences.

In order to successfully address the needs of our students, we must make a commitment to developing culturally responsive teaching behaviors. Culturally- responsive teachers specifically acknowledge the presence of culturally-diverse students and the need for these students to find relevant and positive connections between their experiences and the subject matter (Montgomery 2001). Culturally-responsive teachers also consider the appropriateness of instructional activities for individual students based on their cultural histories. Part of making connections to students' needs and interests is anticipating how their different histories may affect the ways in which they interpret or respond to classroom assignments. The story shared at the beginning of this chapter presented the teacher with an opportunity to learn about how the student was feeling with respect to the assignment given. In a culturally-responsive learning environment, the student in question would feel comfortable to share his feelings about the assignment with his teacher and peers. The insight provided by the student could then be used to guide a student-generated classroom discussion. It is important that we do not let our fear of being perceived as biased or prejudiced keep us from leading our students toward having difficult conversations. It is, indeed, these open and honest conversations that provide us with much needed information about our students' histories, fears, hopes and viewpoints.

> ➤ **Culturally-Responsive Teaching: An Ongoing Process**

In order to dramatically increase student achievement, it is critical that we are relentless in our attempt to provide students with culturally-relevant learning experiences. This is accomplished when we (1) encourage students to *wrestle with text* while making connections between their personal experiences and the curriculum, (2) get a better handle on what students know by providing them the opportunity to articulate their thinking verbally, and (3) ensure that students are given daily opportunities to provide evidence of their thinking in the form of writing.

In this chapter, I will discuss the instructional strategies and teaching techniques that present us with opportunities to increase student achievement by maximizing our students' intellectual potential. The truth is, however, that we may already be incorporating many culturally compatible elements in our instruction (Educational Research Service 2003). Moving forward, our goal is to be clear about which strategies have proven most beneficial to our students and to add culturally responsive instructional strategies to our toolkits.

> Wrestling with text.

The concept of wrestling with text came to me while watching my two young boys interact with one another. One morning while on the treadmill, I noticed that they began a wrestling match. Because I was listening to my Ipod while running, I could not hear the verbal exchange between the two of them. As a mother, my natural instinct was to cease what I was doing and ask the boys to stop wrestling. Instead, I decided to watch them very carefully. What I observed were two little boys who cared a great deal about one another. They were connecting in a way with which they were very comfortable. What I saw was a lot of laughter, a great deal of emotion, and moments of serious thinking about what move (or strategy) should be tried next. I must admit, I did see some tickling going on as well. And then it hit me that this is exactly what we want to see happening in our classrooms. We want our students to be actively engaged in the learning process by wrestling with text as opposed to serving as mere spectators watching a movie. Students should recognize their potential to serve as the leading roles in a stage play. They should think about the wrestling moves (strategies) they are using and why they are using them. Their responsibility is to *act* as if their life depended on it. We want our students to be on the lookout for opportunities to connect to every aspect of their academic experiences by asking themselves, "How is this particular topic, concept or unit of study relevant to my life? Why is this important to me?

Our students have the intellectual capability needed to expand their thinking by exploring viewpoints and questioning an author's perspective. In order for them to take the risk needed to do so we must create healthy learning environments that foster and support their growth and development. In essence, our goal is to assist students in viewing learning as the act of wrestling with concepts. Much like dancing, wrestlers have the ability to control the tempo. In this chapter, I address the concept of wrestling with text by focusing our attention on two big ideas in particular: (1) the importance of student talk and (2) the need for us to develop our students' ability to articulate their thoughts in the form of writing. I address these two elements by breaking them apart and forming smaller focus areas. Yet the two global focuses remain the same. We want our students to become vigorously engaged in conversation and the act of writing on a daily basis.

➢ Opportunities to Talk

Talk is the central tool of our students' trade. With it, they mediate activity and experience. It helps them make sense of learning, literacy, life and themselves. (Johnston 2004). In our attempts to develop our students' literacy abilities, we must recognize that reading and writing, as important as they are, don't replace the need for the vital and ongoing thought and emotion of face-to-face dialogue (Schmoker 2006). It has been my observation that 80% of the academic day is spent in "teacher-talk mode" and 20% or less of a school day is spent in "student-talk mode." I would suggest that we reverse this trend to consist of students spending 80% of the school day engaged in academic dialogue. Doing so decreases the likelihood that we are counterproductive in our pursuit to develop our students' intellectual capabilities. Additionally, we will develop a better understanding of our students' thought processes. Student talk provides valuable information that can be used to assist us in planning instructional experiences that match students' interest levels.

Thinking out loud benefits students because (1) they are better able to demonstrate their ability to bring appropriate background knowledge about reading content to the reading task, (2) use existing life knowledge to make sense of new information, and (3) apply what they are learning to their own questions and concerns (Wilhelm 2007). Studies show that students are most successful at learning new reading and writing strategies and working through the new challenges posed by more difficult genres when they are reading and writing to do work and answer questions that are real and important to them (Wilhelm 2007). While reading, we don't want our students to automatically accept the viewpoint of the author. Instead they should recognize that stories are told from a perspective and that other perspectives are not equally represented (Johnston 2004). The student that was asked to pretend as if he were in the Civil War was confused as to which perspective he was being asked to take. He questioned if he was supposed to pretend as if he were White or represent the perspective of the African-Americans involved in the Civil War. In this case, I would like to contend that all of the students would have benefited from serving as a representative of both perspectives.

Ultimately we want to empower our students by encouraging them to wrestle with text by articulating their thoughts, considering different perspectives and asking critical questions within the context of the classroom. It is important for us to understand that this is something that may not happen naturally for all of our students. Our role is to model the process for them as often as possible.

➤ The Power of Questioning

Teachers play a critical role in arranging the discursive histories from which our children speak. Therefore, we have to ask ourselves what discursive histories have made it possible to say what they say? (Miller 2010). The most effective way to accomplish this goal is by posing thought-generating questions throughout our lessons. There is little in language more fundamental to the formal learning process than the use of questions (Pransky 2008). It is important to recognize however, that there are profound differences among cultures in the use of questions, who is responsible for them, and when to use them. Questions are one of our primary teaching tools; so we must be sensitive to the various nuances questions have within the classroom community and the different ways that our culturally diverse students may respond to them (Pransky 2008).

➤ Questioning to engage culturally-diverse students

Typically, we limit our students' comprehension by asking literal, right-there-in-the-text questions that require only shallow reading and understanding. Common examples are comprehension questions posed by computerized reading-incentive programs and chapter questions in many content area books (Miller 2010). The computerized tests the students take focus on low-level comprehension (trivial details) instead of important ideas and critical thinking. If students read one or two or even three books and answer low-level questions afterward, it might not do much good, but there's no real harm done. But if answering those questions becomes a routine, consistent, ongoing, and integral part of students' reading lives, there can be unintended and negative habits developed. Students may come to believe that the purpose of reading is to focus on unimportant details so they can answer questions on the computer. Thus, they will be trained to read superficially (Gorman 2007).

It is possible for us to assist our students in developing critical thinking skills by asking them guiding (as oppose to literal) questions? An appropriate response to this question is yes. Jeffrey Wilhelm provides us with ten tips for developing the types of questions that can prove beneficial in our attempts to engage our culturally diverse students in the reading process. In order to accomplish this goal, Wilhelm suggests that we reframe existing curricula with guiding questions (Wilhelm 2007). I have carefully selected three of his ten tips for you to consider. These tips serve as a foundation for creating a richer reading experience for all of our students.

Tip One: Reframe a required standard, topic, or text so it matters. For example, if we are required to teach the Civil War, we could ask questions such as, Was the Civil War necessary? Would slavery have disappeared in an acceptable way anyway? We could also ask a question such as, "Is war ever necessary?" Of course, in asking such questions, we must include and respect the viewpoints of students from the various different cultures represented in our classrooms.

Tip Two: Consider the heart of the matter. Brainstorm what is most essential for the students to know, understand and have the ability to do when they have completed a unit of study. Standards documents in language arts often require that students should understand the basic elements of story structure such as character, plot, and setting. Typically teachers define these elements and students will repeat the information on a test. In order to further develop our students as thinkers it is imperative that we recognize that character is defined by a person's responses to problems with which she or he is faced.

An example of questions that would get at the essence of character and plot might be: "How do people reveal their essential character?" Other examples are: How does setting influence and limit character action?" "How does our culture shape and limit our beliefs and actions?"

Tip Three: Ask ethical or moral questions that require judgment about particular concepts, issues or the pursuit of particular kinds of knowledge. Questions that require judgment might include: "What would be a misuse of knowledge?" "Is it ever right to resist an established government?" "Are there conditions in which it is permissible to lie, steal, or cheat (Wilhelm, 2007)? It is useful here for the teacher to be humble and share that even teachers may not have complete and satisfying answers to these fundamental questions. This admission frees the student from searching for a right answer that agrees with the teacher's judgments.

In a culturally-responsive learning environment, students are encouraged to do what Zimmermann and Hutchins refer to as "go public with their learning" (Zimmermann and Hutchins 2003). There are tremendous benefits in students responding to thought-provoking guiding questions. Furthermore, in our attempt to develop the cultural competencies of our students, we should encourage them take advantage of the opportunity to gain insight in to the views and perspectives of peers whose cultural background and experiences may differ from their own.

> **Student-Generated Questions**

In addition to the role that teachers should play in sparking discussion in the classroom, authors Beck and McKeown suggest that we should teach students how to expand their own thinking by engaging in the "Question the Author" (or the QtA.) process while reading (Beck and McKeown 2006). The goal of a QtA discussion is to assist students in developing meaning. Therefore, the discussion takes place in the course of reading the text for the first time so students can share in the experience of how to build meaning from text. Beck and McKeown share with us that the teacher is right there the whole time, as a facilitator, guide, initiator and responder.

In a QtA lesson, students are prompted to interact with the text and converse about it through queries. Perhaps the most typical patterns of traditional classroom discussion are that students tend to report information from a text. Because students are engaged in retrieval of acquired facts and opinions, participation may be flat. In contrast, Beck and McKeown share with us, students in a QtA discussion are expected and encouraged to develop, connect, and explain ideas from a text, not just report information. The ultimate goal of QtA is for students to incorporate these strategies into their own independent reading processes. (Beck and McKeown 2006). We owe it to our students to help them progress beyond mere retrieval of information. Good queries will help them achieve this progress into higher levels of thought.

Isabel Beck and Margaret McKeown provide us with an explanation as to the difference between the purposes of the traditional questioning process and the process of posing queries.

A Comparison of Traditional and Question-the-Author Queries	
Questions:	**Queries:**
➢ Assess student comprehension of test information after the fact.	➢ Assist student with developing the meaning of text ideas in the course of reading.
➢ Focus on teacher-to-student interactions, which generate individual students' responses that the teacher can evaluate.	➢ Facilitate group discussion about author's ideas and encourage student-to-student and student-to-teacher interactions.
➢ Are used before or after reading.	➢ Are used during initial reading.

Figure 1.3 (Beck and McKeown 2006)

In order for us to help our students develop the self-confidence needed to pose effective questions while reading independently, we must carefully monitor their ability to do so. It is equally important to keep in mind the fact that our students may be reading for the purpose of answering a question. This is done to find an answer to specific questions that the reader might have.

Students may also engage in the process of reading with a more general question in mind. This is done to expand student thinking and answer questions of intense personal interest to individual students (Harvey and Goudvis 2007).

The following questions help us to obtain information about how the questioning process is working for our students: (1) "Did you have a question even before you started to read this book?" (2) "How is asking questions working for you?" (3) "How does that question affect your understanding of the story?" (4) "Do you notice yourself asking questions when the reading content doesn't make sense?" (5) "You've stopped to ask a question about the meaning of a word. Is that word keeping you from understanding?" "How will you figure out its meaning (Zimmermann and Hutchins 2003)?"

> **Leaving Tracks of Thinking**

Many of us can recall a time when we became extremely focused while reading to answer a question or with a question in mind. While engaged in the process we naturally began to highlight key points, write notes in the margins, or underline the statements that support our thinking. Ironically, far too often if our students begin to write their thoughts in their textbooks, a teacher might quickly respond by reminding the student that he or she is not permitted to write in the book. I contend that writing in the book is exactly what students have to do in order to keep a track record of their thinking.

I can appreciate this idea now that I am in the process of completing this book. While combing my home library to find books that supported my line of thinking, I discovered that I had written in the margins of each text. The books also contained several pages of highlighted materials and annotations represented in the form of sticky notes. The natural process that I used to leave a track record of my thinking proved beneficial as I perused each text in search of theoretical justification for several of the points expressed throughout this book. While reviewing my notes, it dawned on me that I started writing this book long before I actually engaged in the formal writing process. I then immediately questioned how we can expect our students to transfer their thinking into the form of writing if they are given limited opportunities to engage in the process of what is described by Harvey and Goudvis as leaving tracks of their thinking (Harvey and Goudvis 2007).

There are many strategies that can be used to assist students in recording their thoughts in a meaningful and useful way. I am not suggesting that we rush in to the workrooms located in our schools and run off large copies of our students' textbooks. In fact, the act of doing so in not permitted by textbook companies. I am recommending that we (1) decide the reading focus for each literacy lesson, (2) work with students to determine which portions of the text help them to answer a question and (3) use those portions of the text for the purpose of leaving tracks of their thinking. It is important to remember that after the goal of a lesson has been accomplished, we want our students to have easy access to their notes for the purpose of using them during the writing process.

➢ **Facts, Questions and Response**

In addition to writing in the margins of a piece of text, students can also be introduced to a Facts, Questions and Response (FQR) think-sheet which works to help them organize their thoughts, make sense of, and leave a track-record of their thinking. Stephanie Harvey and Anne Goudvis share with us that the FQR process serves as an outstanding tool for guiding students through the thinking-while-reading process. While reading a piece of text students are encouraged to make note of *facts* that are most important to them (Harvey and Goudvis 2007). This process benefits culturally diverse students because it draws upon their personal experiences and allows them to connect to text by identifying aspects of their reading that they deem most important.

The second step in the process is for students to make note of any *questions* that have come to mind while reading the text. Students are encouraged to share their thinking by posing their questions for consideration. As they read, they should be involved in a search for the answers to their questions. Lastly, students are asked to record their *responses* or connections made while reading (Harvey and Goudvis 2007). The following processes can also be conducted in pairs. By working with a partner, students are provided with another opportunity to develop their ability to articulate their thinking orally.

< Writing to Provide Evidence of Thinking

"Those who write have a tremendous intellectual advantage over those who don't (Schmoker 2006)." It is important to reiterate the fact that in order to ensure that our students are fully engaged in the writing process, they must have opportunities to talk about text. Talking before writing benefits students because they can hone their ideas and rehearse what they are going to write down or share (Harvey and Goudvis 2007).

Despite the crucial role that writing plays in intellectual development and future success, the research paints a discouraging picture. Researchers Kameenui and Carnier have found that studies concur that there is very little writing instruction actually occurring in our schools (Kameenui and Carnine 1998). Russian philosopher Lev Vgotsky contended that writing has occurred in too narrow a place in school as compared to the enormous role that it plays in children's cultural development (Schmoker 2006). Not only do we want them to write, we want our students to attach an internal motivation to the process of writing (Johnston 2004).

By wrestling with text and articulating their thinking on a regular basis, our students are warming up before they write. The end result is that they are better equipped to engage successfully in the writing process. When students are not provided the opportunity to *warm up,* we are in essence, asking them to *write cold.* As a result, students may be unclear as to how to make a connection between what they have been asked to write about and its relevance to their reading and cultural background experiences. As has been described earlier in this chapter, each of the aforementioned approaches provides students with the opportunity to become emotionally connected to both the reading and writing processes. This emotional or personal connection is desperately needed in order for our students to articulate their thinking effectively in the form of writing.

While working to develop competent writers, it is important that we remain committed to modeling the writing process for our students. To build students' know-how, we have to model, mentor and monitor student performance. When we tell or impart information to our students, they tend to forget much of it within two weeks and practically all of it within two years (Wilhelm 2007). To further support my line of thinking, Pransky, shares with us that three of the four stages of learning described by Vgotsky are the most important for culturally and Linguistically Diverse learners:

The three stages emphasized by Pransky are:

Stage one: The need for a clear, explicit, external model. This may be visual or verbal or involve some other sense. However, a more competent peer or adult must scaffold a clear goal or model externally.

Stage two: The internalization of the model (or concept) by the learner. This stage is a much longer process. The skill of good teaching comes in to play here: one must slowly hand over responsibility for the learning, and ownership of the concept, to the learner, not letting go of everything too fast, yet not holding on too long. Timing is everything here.

Stage three: In the stage of Independence, the student has constructed her or his own meaning of the model, the learning goal, or concept and is able to accomplish a task successfully with minimal support (Pransky 2008).

In many cases, our students will develop their writing skills as a result of having constant exposure to models of excellence. Students need to see how a competent adult actually creates lines on a page. Modeling a writing task by talking aloud not only shows the kind of thinking, organizing and explaining that smart writers use but also allows us to lead the way in taking the kinds of risks that we are asking our students to take (Daniels, Zemeleman and Steineke 2007).

Making Writing a Meaningful Experience

Upon a visit to a classroom, it is not at all uncommon to observe students passing notes back and forth. As a classroom teacher, I can still remember my response to such behavior being to request that the students stop writing notes in class. After reflection upon those experiences I now feel that I may have unintentionally discouraged my students from writing. The best way to develop passionate writers is to encourage them to write for multiple purposes (i.e. classroom assignments, essays and notes to classmates) and then ask them to share with us, the types of writing styles with which they are most comfortable. In order to fully engage our students in the writing process, we have to build upon what our students already know and prefer to write about.

Write-Around

To further demonstrate my point, Daniels, Zemelman and Steineke, introduces to us an amazing strategy (referred to as Write-Around) that is much like the writing notes in class process that many of our students love to engage in. In a write-around, a group of three-to-five students write short notes to each other about a rich, complex topic assigned by the teacher. They jot comments, pass their papers, read what the previous student(s) have written, and add their own remarks. The students create a string of conversation as the pages circulate around the table. Each student starts a letter, so at all times everyone is writing (Daniels, Zemelman and Steineke, 2007). An activity of this nature proves extremely beneficial to students from diverse backgrounds because they are able to write for the purpose of providing their own perspectives regarding a topic. Additionally, we send a clear message that validates our commitment to making sure that our students know that their experiences matter.

Culturally-Relevant Writing

In addition to authentic writing, our students have to also be prepared to write for the purposes that have been established via state standards and various curricular expectations. In order for students from diverse backgrounds to be able to demonstrate proficiency in these areas, they must have the opportunity to perfect their writing skills by engaging in Culturally- Relevant Writing activities. In Culturally-Relevant Writing, the teacher selects a topic that is being covered in the curriculum (regardless of the content area), poses a thought-provoking question related directly to the topic, and scaffolds support to students as they write-to-respond to the question. For example, in social studies students may be covering an issue related to social justice. The teacher could pose a question such as "What do you believe is the role of a person who is aware that the rights of someone else have been violated?" Within a pre-specified time frame (30 minutes is recommended), students should then be given an opportunity to articulate their thoughts in the form of writing.

The next step in the process is for teachers to group students into pairs. The students proceed by reading their responses to each another. Each student is then given the opportunity to ask questions in order to clarify her or his partner's thinking. After this has been accomplished, the students are then prompted to react to the written statements by their peers. During the response phase of the process, all students are required to indicate the life experiences have caused them to feel the way that they do about the topic as well as the written responses provided by their peers. Students can indicate whether or not their feelings are a direct match with the feelings articulated by their peers. Some students may consider providing details about why their feelings differ significantly from their peers. This activity is not to be done for the purpose of encouraging students to evaluate or assess their peers' writing ability. Instead, we want our students to make connections by identifying aspects of the topic that are relevant to their lives. The direct result will be that they will become fully engaged in the process of writing, thereby building their stamina for communicating in writing.

In the end, our goal is for students to be able to write for large blocks of uninterrupted time. In order to develop their skills in this area, they must be motivated to write. The link between student motivation and achievement are straightforward. If students are motivated to learn the content in a given subject, their achievement in that subject will most likely be good. If students are not motivated to learn the content, their achievement will likely be limited (Marzano 2003).

Culturally-Relevant Writing Activity
Writing to Increase the Achievement Levels of
Students from Diverse Backgrounds

Step One
Teacher poses a thought-provoking question related directly to the text.

Step Two
Students are asked to respond to the question, adding information about the life experiences that have influenced their thinking about the topic. (Students are responsible for writing uninterruptedly for a minimum of 30 minutes).

Step Three
The teacher plays a dominant role by selecting which students to pair up for the Relevant- Writing Activity. Diversity of thought and perspectives should be considered while grouping students. Each student should be provided with a copy of her or his peer's writing.

Step Four
In pairs, the students read their response to each another. The person that will be responsible for reacting to the writing is given an opportunity to ask questions in order to clarify the writer's thinking. (Students should be given at least 30 minutes to accomplish this task).

Step Five Students are then given a period of 30 minutes to react to their peer's writing. All students are required to indicate the life experiences that have impacted their feelings about the topic.

Figure 1.4

Note- it is recommended that the Culturally-Relevant Writing

Activity be conducted in at least two class periods.

Dramatically Increase Writing Achievement

In order to dramatically increase the writing achievement levels of our students, they should be engaged in the Culturally-Relevant Writing Activity no less than twice weekly. There are multiple benefits of engaging in this process. Our students will naturally develop their writing skills and abilities because (1) they are asked to respond to thought-generating questions as opposed to literal questions (which strengthens their ability to think critically and analytically), (2) they are actively engaged in the process of writing from their own perspective (which validates their experiences and sends a message that they are important), (3) they are responding to the thoughts of their peers (which serves as a great motivator for writing), (4) they are provided the opportunity to think out loud by clarifying their thoughts with their peers (which further demonstrates their competencies and is just plain fun!) and (5) they are gaining a better sense of who their peers are (thereby further developing their cultural competencies).

Engaging in this process allows students to make a smooth transition into the more formulaic writing required of them on many state examinations. In order for students to be able to handle the rigor involved in the types of writing required on standardized tests, they have to feel that they are competent writers. Their confidence is built as they develop the stamina needed to produce a thoughtful piece of writing. Writing about things that matter encourages students to write for longer periods of time. Unfortunately, for too many of our students, the first time that they are asked to write for a lengthy time frame is when they are faced with a standardized test. To make matters worse, the traditional standardized test introduces students to a writing prompt that may or may not have any relevance to their lives (this is very often the case for students from diverse cultural and ethnic backgrounds).

I am not suggesting that we do not need to provide students with exposure to the narrative, expository and persuasive writing processes. I am however suggesting that if we want our students to become passionate writers as well as demonstrate proficiency on state exams, we must develop their competency levels. This is more likely to occur when we allow them to write daily about what actually matters to them. In other words, we must not miss the connection between increasing student achievement in the area of writing, and *the act of writing itself.*

Chapter Four

Ensuring High Levels of Learning For All

"A critical principle of differentiated learning is that all students must meet standards, but they are given materials and activities that help them use their interests and preferred styles in achieving those standards (Whitaker 2012)".

"Our goal is to improve parental involvement by supporting them in their efforts to become better providers for their children (Whitaker 2012)".

Questions that drive this chapter of study:

1. In what ways do gender differences contribute to the achievement gap between male and female students?

2. Is it possible that students have preferred methods for demonstrating what they know and are able to do?

3. What approaches can be implemented for increased parental involvement in our elementary and high schools?

It is not easy to be a culturally-responsive teacher. There are issues and obstacles that must be faced and overcome. These include cultural differences between male and females, the need for balanced assessments, and non-traditional approaches to parental involvement. In this final chapter, I will address techniques for overcoming these obstacles.

GENDER DIFFERENCES

In an important way, male and female cultures are different. Culturally-responsive teaching takes into consideration race, ethnicity, language and also differences in the achievement of males and females. The reality is that across our entire country, male students are being out-performed by female students. In kindergarten, boys and girls do equally well on tests of reading, general knowledge, and mathematics. By third grade, boys have slightly higher mathematics scores and slightly lower reading scores. As children grow older, these gaps widen. Between 9 and 13 years of age, the gender gaps approximately double in science and reading. Between 13 and 17, the gap in science continues to expand but there is little growth in the math or reading gap. The size of the gaps is not trivial. The underperformance of 17-year-old boys in reading is equivalent to 1.5 years of schooling, and though men continue to be over-represented in College Level Science and engineering, girls are now more likely to go to college and persist in earning a degree (Gorman 2012).

I became most aware of how this might occur as a result of an interaction that I had with my oldest son. Because of my commitment to the field of education, I am often attending conferences and returning home with more books than I can fit in one suitcase. My son has always been the lucky recipient of the wonderful books that I was convinced would make a great addition to his home library. Upon returning home from a book summit in New York, I decided to conduct an activity with him in order to make sure that we was indeed engaged in the texts that I would present to him each night. As a warm-up activity, I shared with him that we would begin by categorizing all of the books in his library. He and I spent several hours for about three days off and on working on this initial project. After that, I asked my son to go in to his room and bring out the books in his library that he enjoyed reading. If you are familiar with the saying "Be careful what you ask for," you can certainly appreciate what happened next. After about thirty minutes or so, he came out of his room. Right away, I noticed that he only selected two books. I began to feel a bit uneasy. Therefore, I asked him if he needed help carrying the other books. He replied, "No mom, these are the only books that I like." I asked my son to explain to me why he never told me that he did not find the books that I had been bringing home interesting. My son replied, "Mom, you never asked." I was devastated. After all, over the years, I had spent a significant amount of time building up his home library. I was almost certain that I was doing the right thing. To say that I was hurt would be an understatement.

I immediately became overwhelmed when I began to think about how long I had gone without the critical information provided to me by my son. I then began to reflect on the many nights that I spent sharing with my husband my concern about what appeared to be my son's lack of interest in reading. After having had this experience with my son, I came to realize that he was very much interested in reading. However, I did not take the time to find out about the types of reading material that were of most interest to him. I learned that there was a cultural conflict between the reading interest level of my son and his mother. Very often the same holds true as female teachers interact with their male students daily. So, how do we better explain the gap in achievement between female and male students? Overall, the data suggest that, "A large fraction of boys' dramatic underperformance in reading reflects the classroom dynamics associated with the fact that their reading teachers are overwhelmingly female." According to the U.S. Department of Education's 1999-2000 Schools and Staffing Survey, 91 percent of the nation's sixth-grade reading teachers, and 83 percent of eighth-grade reading teachers are female. This depresses boys' achievement (U.S. Department of Education, 2002).

I would like to contend that we must demonstrate cultural competency by aggressively addressing the negative implications of our curricular decisions, instructional and assessment approaches. We must also weigh the impact of those implications on the achievement levels of our male students.

I am not in any way suggesting that female teachers are unable to provide male students with high-quality learning experiences. I am however, suggesting that in order to do so successfully, we must invite male student perspectives in decisions that affect their ability to succeed in school. With regard to the experience that I had with my son, I could have avoided the cultural conflict that occurred by simply inviting him to share information with me about the types of books that he enjoys reading. It is also important to take into consideration that boys have preferred learning styles and preferred reading materials. Male students tend to prefer reading sports magazines, comic books, books about wrestling and cars as well as other types of non-fiction material. It is also a good idea to put boys who have similar interest together to read and talk about books. If we are to continue to engage our male students in the reading process, our classrooms must reflect their interest levels. One way to accomplish this goal is by allowing boys to have a choice in the book-selection process.

A careful examination of our classroom libraries, lesson plans, curriculum guides and materials will reveal whether or not we are meeting the needs of our male students by providing them with culturally-relevant learning opportunities.

BALANCED ASSESSEMENT

Concern about gender and educational attainment focuses mainly on the extent to which females and males perform differently. In addition to our students' having different interest-levels, they also have preferred methods of demonstrating what they know and are able to do. Recognition of the ways in which students from diverse cultural backgrounds demonstrate what they know can positively impact student learning. Culturally-responsive teachers intentionally implement processes in their classrooms that can be used to identify the interest and preferred delivery methods of their students.

A student who has not demonstrated mastery of the material as is indicated on one particular assessment (such as a standardized test, much like I experienced in school) may have the ability to demonstrate mastery in other ways. Therefore, it is important to implement the use of multiple forms of assessments in our classrooms. Many of us may take into consideration the learning styles that are represented in our classrooms. For example, we may note that some of our students are auditory, visual or kinesthetic learners. Auditory learners perform better with information that they can hear. They tend to talk while they write (much like I am doing at this very moment) and discuss what they are thinking with others. Auditory learners are also very easily distracted. On the other hand, visual learners perform best when they have something to see. They prefer to have charts, graphs and tables presented to them in order to assist them in grasping particular concepts. Kinesthetic learners enjoy hands-on learning experiments. Doing so helps them to comprehend the information presented to them. They also prefer to be constantly moving around and keep their brains busy. We must serve all types of learners.

Again, I would like to expand our thinking to include an examination of the ways in which our students prefer to demonstrate what they know and are able to do. In order to accomplish this task we should begin by providing students with an explanation of available possibilities, and then ask them to identify their own learning styles.

It is necessary for students to have an understanding of their learning styles in order to develop a better appreciation for teacher delivery styles that will be most effective. For example, I am auditory learner and I prefer to demonstrate what I know by speaking orally. This is a strength that I have. However, during my school-aged experiences my teachers consistently issued fill-in-the-blank assessments. As a result, they were unable to gain an accurate sense of my intellectual capabilities. By providing me with the opportunity to identify which assessment style most appropriately matched my preferred delivery method, my teachers would have gained the information needed to make the necessary adjustments to their instruction.

In the case of visual learners, they may prefer to demonstrate what they know by conducting a presentation to include charts, graphs, paintings and other artifacts, which can be used to further demonstrate their mastery of a particular standard or objective.

Another student in your class that has a kinesthetic learning style may prefer to demonstrate what he or she knows by physically moving around in order to demonstrate proficiency. An effective way to address this need is by affording this type of student with the opportunity to participate in a hands-on scientific experiment or producing a product that could then be demonstrated to others. They key is to balance our assessments by giving students "a choice in the matter." Of course, the ultimate outcome must be that the students are able to meet the externally imposed challenge of standardized tests, but this may not be the appropriate first step.

A critical principle of differentiated learning is that all students must meet standards, but they are given materials and activities that help them use their interests and preferred styles in achieving those standards. Teaching and assessment must be appropriately coordinated. The job of teaching includes both appropriate instruction and assessment.

I want to emphasize that we do not serve our students well unless they can perform well on the standardized tests that so heavily influence their life chances in the future. We have an obligation to help our students to be able to fare well on standardized tests. This is absolutely necessary if they are to achieve fairness in the choices that will be made about their applications for employment and continued education. We live in a system and in a society that emphasizes meeting standards and using standardized tests. We must send out our students prepared to meet these challenges. We cannot afford to throw away any test (including standardized tests). Our challenge is to find ways to use these tests well and to use them in balance with other forms of assessment (Stiggins 1994).

Culturally-relevant teaching and assessment require both appropriate use of summative assessment, which is usually in the form of standardized tests, as well as excellent use of formative assessment. Summative assessment is an assessment of learning, a tool to answer the question, "Did the students learn by the deadline?" with a "yes" or "no," "pass" or "fail," "proficient" or "not" (Dufour, Dufour and Eaker, 2008). Formative assessment is an assessment for learning, a tool to be used to provide information to the teacher and the student about the student's current level of achievement and what steps should be taken next to improve student learning (Dufour, Dufour and Eaker, 2008).

While large-scale standardized tests may have great influence at specific times, without question, teachers are the drivers of the assessment systems that determine the effectiveness of schools (Stiggins 1994). Therefore, we must be relentless in our efforts to incorporate the use of formative assessments that most appropriately match our students' preferred methods of demonstrating what they know and are able to do. This is critical in that the purpose of assessment is to gain insight in to what our students know, relevant to the standards, and make the necessary adjustments in instruction. If there is no change in how we deliver instruction, based on what we learn about our students, they may only achieve minimal results. We really need to look at assessment from the perspective of teacher instruction with regard to constant monitoring of student learning and data from what happens after we obtain student-learning results.

One of the most consistent findings from research on effective schools and effective teaching is the power of frequent monitoring of student learning (Dufour, Dufour & Eaker 2008). The effective use of authentic formative assessments is particularly helpful because this allows us to access information about student learning from multiple data points to include portfolio measures and samples of student work. The results of performance assessments such as student proficiency in the areas of the arts, sciences, dramatic performances, physical activities and computer technology are also initial points of entry into the concepts which will eventually be assessed by summative (or standardized) tests. In short, we must start where students are but we must take them where they need to be.

Non-Traditional Approaches for Increased Parental Involvement

Just as male and female cultures are different, teacher and parent cultures can be very different as well. Therefore, it is imperative that we include parents in our concept of culturally-relevant teaching. In other words, we must address and show respect for parents of all cultural backgrounds. Teachers and parents share a common goal. That goal is success for students of all cultural backgrounds. We can accomplish this goal is by considering non-traditional approaches to increased parental involvement.

Non-traditional approaches are particularly helpful during our current economy. Far too many parents and guardians (from various economic backgrounds) are finding themselves either unemployed or burnt-out physically and emotionally as a result of working overtime to meet the needs of their families. If schools are going to see improved student learning, we must address the immediate needs of the parents. In other words, we must carefully consider the implications of societal ills on our work as professional educators. To further elaborate on my point, I would like to share the following example for consideration:

In my role as district administrator, I recognized that we were in need of increased parental involvement. I began to examine the practices that we were implementing in order to reach our mission. It is only after careful analysis that I realized that our approaches were very traditional. Like most school districts, bi-annually, we hosted our parent teacher conferences. Parents were asked to report to the school in order to obtain information about the progress of their children. Our parent-teacher conferences were strategically scheduled to occur shortly after the district-level assessment had been issued so that teachers would have recent assessment results for individual students, which could then been shared with the parents. On other occasions, we would host events such as family-reading night, math nights and family-fun nights. Parent turnout had not been ideal in any of these situations.

Again, after thoughtful reflection, it dawned on me that perhaps we should consider reasons why parents were not in attendance. After doing so, the following thought ran through my mind, which I would like for you to consider:

If you have ever taken an airplane flight, you might recall that at the beginning of takeoff, the flight attendant announces, "In the event of an unlikely emergency, the adults are asked to reach for the oxygen mask (which will drop from the ceiling) and place it over your nose and mouth." Secondly, the adults on the plane are then informed that if they are traveling with children, they should repeat the process with them. In essence, the adults are prompted to take care of themselves so that they will be adequately equipped to take care of their children. Unfortunately, in schools we have implemented what I refer to as an upside-down model in our attempt to increase parental involvement. It is with this thought process in mind that I suggest that, in our effort to increase parental involvement dramatically, it is imperative that we make a commitment to find out how to support parents.

In an attempt to address this issue, in my role as a school district official, we elected to host Parent- Literacy Nights. The purpose of these events was to invite parents to come to the school so that we could provide them with specific details as to how they could increase their students' literacy achievement. Each session started out with parents and students eating a catered dinner together at the school. The students were then escorted to various classrooms and received grade-appropriate literacy instruction from local university professors and graduate students. During the same time frame, parents were given explicit instruction as to what they could do at home to support their students in reaching the literacy goals that were established for them. This is key. I have found that far too often, parents receive only very general information about how to support their children's learning in the home setting. The problem with a more general approach is that if the student is in need of significant improvement, for example, in the area of reading comprehension, asking the child to read to their parents every night may not give us the type of drastic improvement needed in the optimal amount of time. Therefore, more explicit instruction to the parent is needed. To further elaborate on this example, we might ask the parent to begin by asking his or her child to read shorter amounts of text and answer critical-thinking questions (perhaps that we have provided) and then move on to increasing the amount of text exposure as their child begins to demonstrate proficiency.

During the final phase of the first Family-Literacy Night, parents were invited into the computer lab. This was done as a result of several parents expressing to me a concern about their lack of ability to complete on-line applications for jobs. Once again, after deep reflection, it dawned on me that we needed to support the parents so that they would be better able to support the learning of their children. Therefore, during their time in the computer lab, the parents received direct training on how to access and navigate the Internet. We also engaged in a question-and-answer session, which afforded the parents the opportunity to ask questions related to their job search interests.

In thinking ahead, schools can further expand opportunities for parents by collaborating with local agencies to host job fairs for the parents. In preparation for the job fairs, the parents could engage in a series of practice interviews right on the school campus. Thinking of this nature could cause some to question whether or not it is the role of the school to support parents in the manner in which I am suggesting. My response to this line of thinking is that the success of our students is inherently wrapped up in our willingness to incorporate non-traditional approaches to supporting their parents. In doing so, we develop a close bond with parents. The end result is that parents will not view the school as an intimidating place to visit and converse about their students' weaknesses, but rather a place that is committed to supporting them in their efforts to become better providers for their children.

This will quite naturally lend itself to parents becoming better able to support their children's learning. When parents are frustrated by not being able to fill out an application on-line for example, they are least likely to be able to remain focused on supporting their children in school. This is especially true, when they haven't been able to meet their own needs or put on their own oxygen masks. We can help our students by enabling parents to give the appropriate time to the progress and development of their children. I am suggesting that we demonstrate cultural responsiveness when we respond to the needs of our students' parents. As was demonstrated in Chapter One of this book, in the Peoria, Illinois school, the non-traditional approach to parent-teacher conferences ultimately resulted in the teachers learning more about the special interests and unique qualities of their students and their families.

In closing, while reading this book, you may have recognized that I chose not to directly address various political hot topics such as No Child Left Behind (NCLB), Adequate Yearly Progress (AYP), Common Core State Standards, Response to

Intervention (RTI), and Race to The Top Initiatives. There are several books and policy reports that adequately address the aforementioned topics. My goal is to support teachers during this very difficult time in public education by further emphasizing how important it is that we remain focused on our true calling. We entered teaching in order to be helpful to students of all cultural backgrounds. Let us discuss and, if necessary, adapt the above-mentioned initiatives, in order to focus our efforts on achieving success for students, teachers, and parents/guardians of all races, languages, and genders.

This book is intended to give us techniques and strategies by which we can achieve specific objectives while holding fast to the values that led us to teaching in the first place. The truth is: there is no "one size fits all" and no one strategy that works best for all students. Therefore, we must continue our commitment to learn from one another, learn from our students and learn from their parents. Together we can make a difference.

The bottom line is this: Our success with our students is dependent upon the extent to which we believe that we can improve the life chances for each of them.

REFERENCES

Beck I. & McKeown. G. (2006). *Improving Comprehension With Questioning the Author: A Fresh and Expanded View of a Powerful Approach*. New York, NY. Scholastic.

Collins, J. (2001). *Why Some Companies Make the Leap and Others Don't: Good to Great*. New York, NY. Harper Collins Publishing Inc.

Covey, S. (2004). *The 8th Habit: From Effectiveness to Great*. New York, NY. Free Press.

Cross, W.E. (1991). *Shades of Black: Diversity In African American Identity*. Philadelphia. Temple University Press.

Daniels, S., Zemelman, S. and Steineke, N. (2007). *Content Area Writing*. Portsmouth, NH. Heinemann Publishing.

Dufour R., Dufour R. & Eaker, R. (2008). *Revisiting Professional Learning Communities at Work: New Insights for Improving Schools*. Bloomington, IN. Solution Tree.

Editorial Projects in Education, "Diplomas Count 2010: Graduating by Number: Putting Data to Work for Student Success," special issue, *Education Week* 29, no.34 (2010).

Educational Research Service (2003). *What We Know About: Culture and Learning*. Alexandria, Virginia: Educational Research Service.

Garcia, G. E., & Willis, A. I. (2001). Frameworks for understanding multicultural literacies. In P .R. Schmidt and P.B. Mosenthal (Eds.), *Reconceptualizing literacy in the new age of multiculturalism and pluralism* (3-31). Greenwich, CT: Information Age Publishing.

Gorman, L. (2012). *Teachers and the Gender Gap*. The National Bureau of Economic Research. Cambridge, MA.

Kameenui E.J. and Carnine D.W. (1998). *Effective Teaching Strategies That Accommodate Diverse Learners*. Upper Saddle River, NJ. Merrill.

Marzano, B. (2003). *What Works in Schools. Translating Research into Action*. Alexandria, Virginia. Association for Supervision and Curriculum Development.

Miller, D. (2010). "Changing Stories: Trajectories of Identification Among African-American Youth in a Science Outreach Apprenticeship." *American Educational Research Journal*. December 2010. 47(4). 879-918.

Montgomery, W. (2001). "Creating-Culturally Responsive, Inclusive Classrooms." *Teaching Exceptional Children* March/April:4-9.

National Women's Law Center (2007). *When Girls Don't Graduate, We All Fail: A Call to Improve High School Graduation Rates for Girls*. Washington, D.C. www.nwlc.org.

Nelson. S., and Guerra, P. (2007). Cultural Proficiency. *National Staff Development Council*. 28(4).

Pransky. K. (2008). *Beneath The Surface: The Hidden Reality of Teaching Culturally and Linguistically Diverse Young Learners k-6*. Portsmouth, NH. Heinemann Publishing.

Routman, R. (2003). *Reading Essentials: The Specifics You Need to Teach Reading Well*. Portsmouth, NH. Heinemann Publishing.

Schmoker, M. (2006). *Results Now: How We Can Achieve Unprecedented Improvements In Teaching and Learning*. Alexandria, Virginia. Association for Supervision and Curriculum Development.

Stiggins R. (2005). Assessment for Learning: Building a Culture of Confident Learners. In DuFour, R., DuFour, R., and Eaker, On

Common Ground: The Power of Professional Learning Communities. Bloomington. ID. Solution Tree.

Tatum, B. (2003). *Why Are All The Black Kids Sitting Together in the Cafeteria? And Other Conversations About Race*. New York, NY. Perseus Books Group.

U.S. Department of Education. (May 2002). *Schools and Staffing Survey, 1999-2000: Overview of the Data for Public, Private, Public Charter, and Bureau of Indian Affairs Elementary and Secondary Schools*.

U.S. Department of Education, National Center for Education Statistics, *Digest of Education Statistics* 2009 (NCES 2010-013) (Washington, DC: U.S. Government Printing Office, 2010).

Vygotsky, L. (1986). *Thought and Language.* Cambridge, Massachusetts Institute of Technology Press.

Whitaker, S. (2010). *The Culturally-Responsive Teacher: How Understanding Culture Positively Impacts Instruction and Student Achievement*. Portsmouth, NH. Heinemann Publishing.

Zimmerman, S. and Hutchins, C. (2003). *7 Keys to Comprehension: How to Help Your Kids Read It and Get It!* New York: Three Rivers Press.

ABOUT THE AUTHOR

Dr. Sonya L. Whitaker currently serves as Superintendent in Lockport, Illinois. In her role she is responsible for establishing and maintaining the fiscal health of the school district, increasing the academic achievement levels of the students, making policy recommendations to the Board of Education, and appropriately allocating financial, technological and human resources to achieve the goal of "Ensuring High Levels of Learning for All." Dr. Whitaker is a published author. In April of 2010, Heinemann Educational publishing company released Dr. Whitaker's professional development DVD entitled: "The Culturally Responsive Teacher: How Understanding Culture Positively Impacts Instruction and Student Achievement."

Dr. Whitaker has experience as a Reading Program Consultant and has served as adjunct professor for National-Louis University in Illinois. She maintains a tireless commitment to expanding her knowledge as a practitioner and as a consumer of research. Dr. Sonya Whitaker has successfully obtained four college degrees in the field of education. Academically, she received the degree of Bachelor of Arts from Clark Atlanta University located in Atlanta, Georgia. Dr. Whitaker's interest in deepening her understanding of the role that educational leadership plays in organizing systems that result in an increase in student achievement, led to her pursuing and successfully obtaining the degrees of Master of Arts in Educational Leadership and Administration from the University of Illinois at Chicago and the Educational Specialist and Doctor of Education Degrees from Northern Illinois University.

Prior to her appointment to the position of Superintendent she served as a central office administrator for the largest elementary school district in the state of Illinois. At the district level, she held the titles of Director for Academic Improvement and Director of Literacy. In those positions she was responsible for coordinating curriculum, instruction, assessment and implementing research-based professional development opportunities for literacy coaches, reading specialists, principals and classroom teachers. Dr. Whitaker is a national speaker and she has provided consultation in the form of keynote presentations and town hall think-tank discussions to educators, politicians, community and faith-based organizations in Atlanta, Chicago, Boston, Milwaukee, Kentwood and Benton Harbor, Michigan, San Diego, Los Angeles and Palm Springs, California.

Use this page to engage in thoughtful reflection.